D1243197

THE STORY OF

GLASS

Bottles and Containers Through the Ages

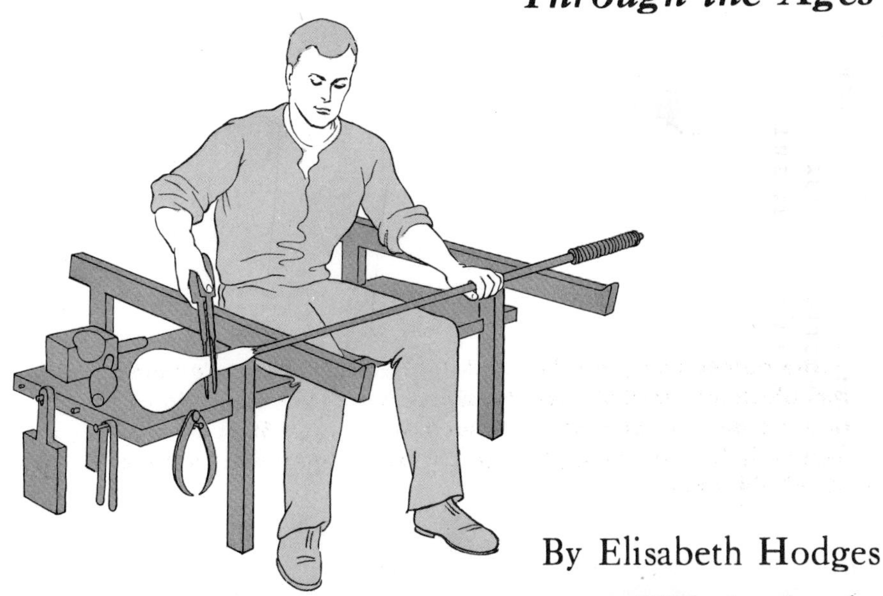

By Elisabeth Hodges

With drawings by
James L. McCreery

STERLING PUBLISHING CO., Inc., NEW YORK
MAYFLOWER • London

BOOKS IN THIS SERIES

The Story of Clocks
The Story of Glass
The Story of Houses
The Story of Maps
The Story of Rivers
The Story of Schools
The Story of Stations

The author and publisher wish to thank the Glass Container Manufacturers Institute for its invaluable cooperation. Thanks also are due to Baccarat & Porthault, Inc. and to Steuben Glass especially for supplying photographs and information on pages 42, 43, 44 and 48.

419 Fourth Avenue, New York 16, N. Y.
Manufactured in the United States of America
Library of Congress Catalog Card No.: 60-14349

CONTENTS

THE STORY OF GLASS

Everyone uses glass. People all over the world use it every day in many ways. It is so much a part of our lives that we take it for granted. Stop and think for a minute. What would happen if all the glass suddenly vanished from the earth? Just imagine your home without windows, or lights, or bottles and jars. How uncomfortable you would be! Think of all the food, medicines and soft drinks that would be missing. Industry and transportation would stop, too. Even great telescopes and reflecting mirrors would be gone, and thousands of persons would be unable to see without glasses.

Glass is an amazing substance. It can be spun into the finest thread or blown into a fragile ornament for your Christmas tree. It can be made so tough and strong that it will stop a bullet or build a skyscraper. Some glass is so clear that you hardly know it is there. Other glass is made so that you cannot see through it. It can be molded or blown into almost any shape, and it comes in every color of the rainbow.

THE EARLIEST GLASS

Natural Glass

Glass was being made on earth long before man existed. Then, as still happens today, it was made by new and fiery volcanoes. Rocks

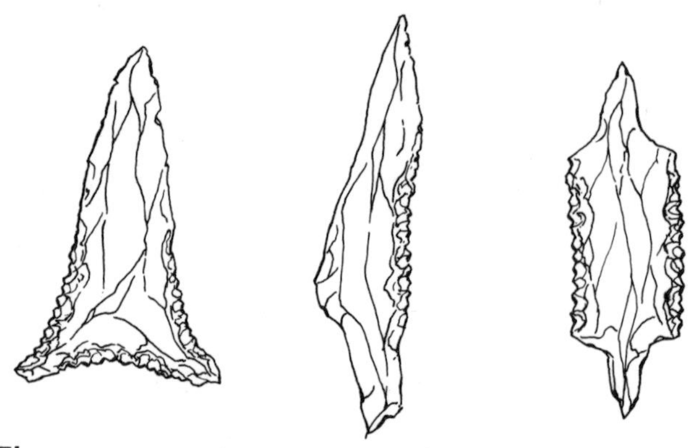

These are arrowheads and spearheads of obsidian, made by cave men.

containing "silica" (a pure form of sand) were melted into lava. The molten lava poured over the sides of the volcanoes, and cooled into a form of glass called "obsidian." Early cave men discovered this hard, glassy material and chipped it into very sharp knives and arrowheads.

The Legend Concerning the Phoenicians

Though glass is the oldest manufactured substance on earth, no one knows for certain when man discovered how to make it. Pliny, the Roman historian of the first century A.D., told an interesting story of its beginnings in the days of the early Phoenicians.

The Phoenicians were well established by 1250 B.C. as a fearless seafaring people and a nation of great merchants. They sailed over seas and along great rivers where others dared not go to trade oils, perfumes, spices and minerals among the nations of the Old World.

One day, a trading ship was returning home along the coast of Syria with a cargo of natron which is a form of baking soda. The crew was hungry and decided to land, cook dinner and, perhaps, stay over night. Gathering a great pile of driftwood for a fire, the men looked around for rocks to build a fireplace. The smooth, sandy beach was bare. There was not a rock to be seen anywhere! What would they do? How could they support their cooking pot? Suddenly one of the sailors pointed to the boat. He had an idea! Why not use a few blocks of natron?

Everyone agreed. Hastily the men went to the ship and brought back pieces of the mineral. In no time at all they had built a rough fireplace, and soon dinner was cooking over a hot fire.

After eating, the men sat around the fire spinning tales of their adventures. A cool breeze began to blow, and they piled more fuel on the fire. Higher and higher leaped the flames. The heat felt good! One by one, the men grew sleepy and dozed.

When they awoke the fire was out, and it had turned cold. One of the sailors poked the ashes, hoping to stir up a fire. Something in the heap was glittering! He bent closer and saw what looked like a tiny river of ice. Excited, he called to the other men, who quickly gathered around the fireplace to examine the strange, shiny stuff. They picked it up, and found that it was hard. What was it, they wondered, and how did it get there? Carefully the men carried it to the boat and took it home with them. Everyone admired the new substance, but for a long time it remained a mystery. No one seemed to know what it was.

Later it was discovered that the hot fire had melted the clean beach sand and the soda together to form glass. And from that time on, so the story goes, man has known the secret of making glass. Scientists doubt that this story is true because, although glass is made by melting soda and sand (silica) together, it takes much more heat than an ordinary cooking fire can produce. There is no doubt, however, that the first glass was somehow made quite by accident.

The First Man-Made Glass

The first man-made glass that we know about was made in Mesopotamia, an ancient country of Asia which is included in modern Iraq. This glass was green and in the form of a glaze was used to cover stone beads. Some of these beads were found in Egypt. They are unbelievably old—*14,000 years!*

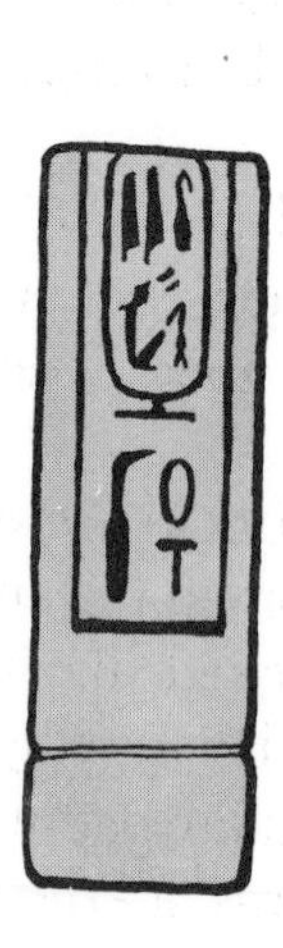

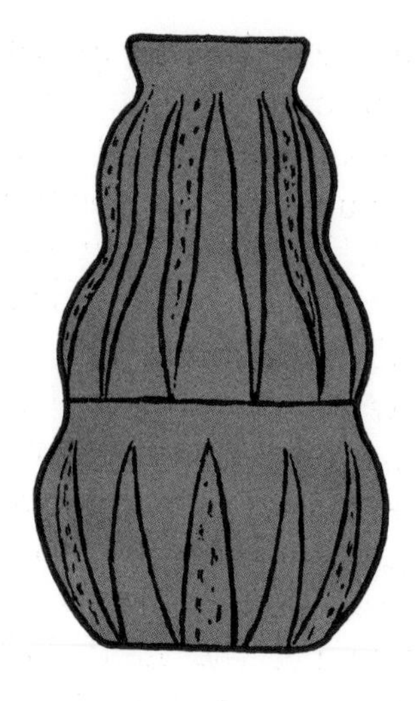

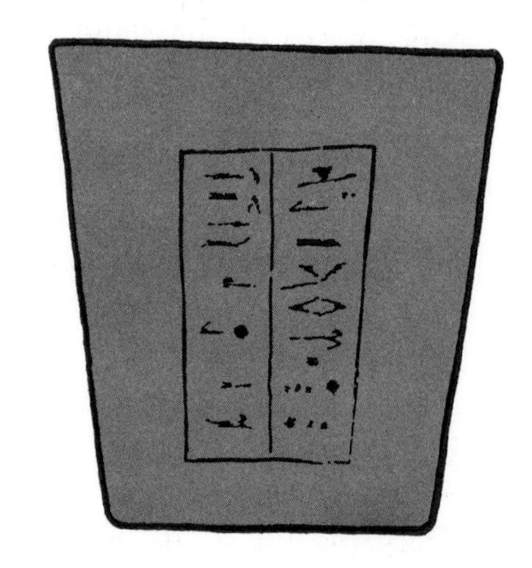

Here are some pieces of glazed stoneware from ancient Mesopotamia and Egypt. At the time they were made, perhaps as long as 6,000 years ago, men did not yet know how to make solid glass.

People went on making glazed stone beads for a long time. Finally, about 5,000 years later, someone found out how to make solid glass beads by building up layers and layers of glaze.

Glass in Egypt

The Egyptians were the first to make real glass bottles and jars. These containers were small and brightly colored. Royalty and persons of wealth used them for perfume, cosmetics and ointments. Although it may seem strange to us, they were also used to hold tears! When a king or other important person died, mourners cried into the tiny tear bottles, which were then buried in the tomb. Our museums have many of these little Egyptian bottles. In fact, the oldest one of all is in the Corning Museum of Glass in Corning, New York. This bottle, made about 3,500 years ago, is only four inches high.

This tiny bottle is only four inches high. It was made in Egypt about 3,500 years ago.

Glassmaking was slow work in those early times. First the glassmaker built a "core" or mold of clay or sand around a metal rod. Then, with great patience, he dipped the core into the molten glass

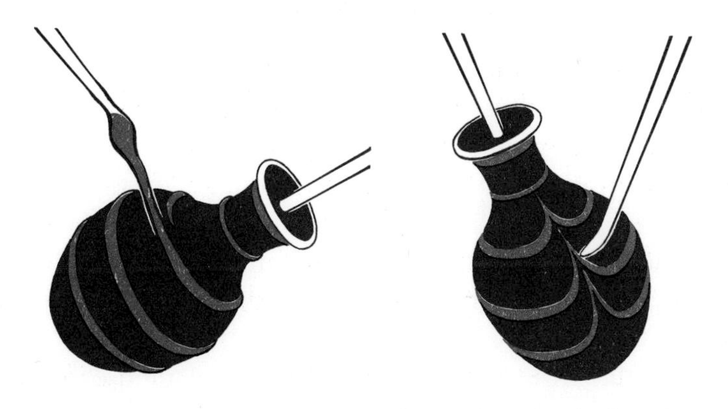

Early bottles were decorated with brightly colored threads of glass. While they were still hot, the threads were trailed on the bottle surfaces and combed into a design.

over and over again. Each layer of glass was shaped by a wooden paddle. When the bottle was thick enough and the right shape, the worker trailed threads of hot glass on the outside. These brightly colored threads were pushed or "combed" into a design. After the bottle had cooled, he took out the rod and carefully scraped out the sand mold. Then he polished the bottle until it shone.

Egyptian glass containers like these were decorated with bright colors.

GLASSMAKING CHANGES

The Invention of the Blowpipe and the Mold

Glass was made slowly in this way for hundreds of years. Then, probably somewhere in Syria during the first century B.C., the blowpipe was invented, and all this was changed. No one knows who thought of the idea. Perhaps a glassmaker put one end of the hollow rod (which he used to dip out the molten material) into his mouth and blew. Puff – a big glass bubble appeared. How surprised he must have been!

To blow glass, the worker dipped the end of the blowpipe into the melted mixture. A small gob of glowing hot glass was gathered and shaped roughly on a marble slab. Then he lifted the pipe and blew through the other end. At the same time he whirled the pipe in big circles to shape the bottle. This took great skill and lung power.

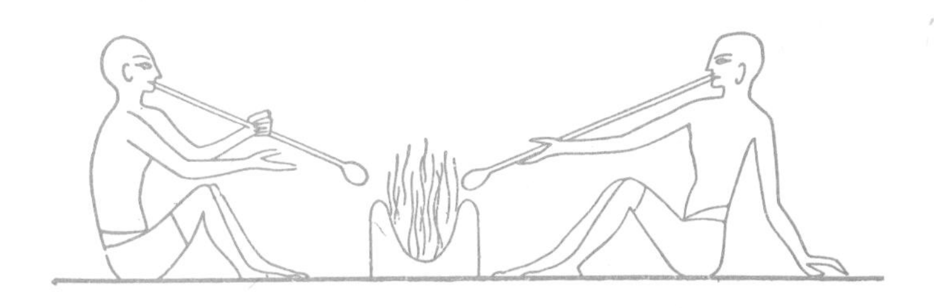

After dipping the end of the blowpipe into molten glass, the glassmaker blew through the other end of the pipe. Hand-blown glass today is made much the same way as it was in early Egypt.

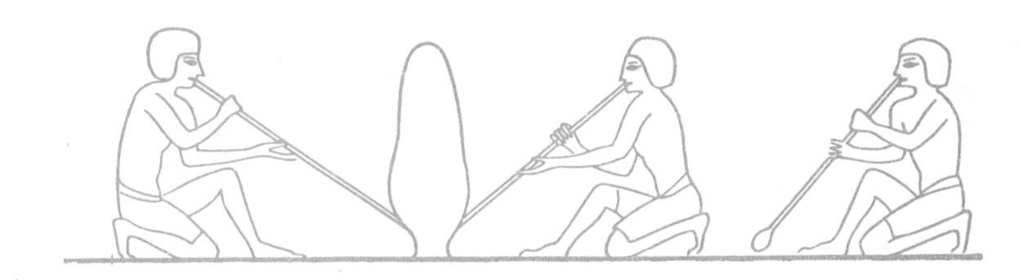

Later, another way of blowing glass was developed. Instead of whirling the pipe in the air, the glassmaker took a few puffs and blew the red-hot glass bubble into a hollow mold to shape it. Mold-blown glass took even less time to make, and the containers were more uniform in size and shape.

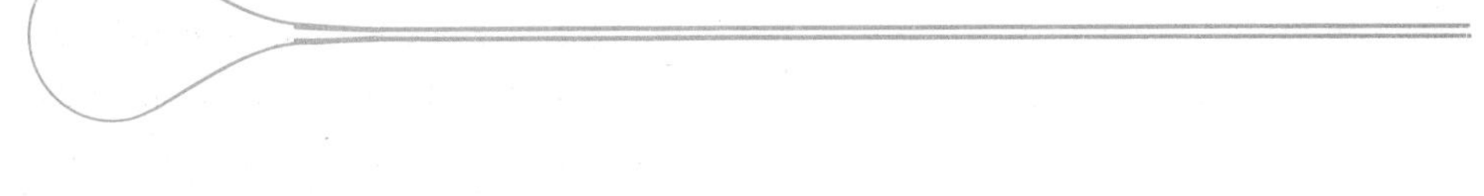

A blowpipe is a hollow iron rod, four to five feet long. One end of it is shaped something like a small bell.

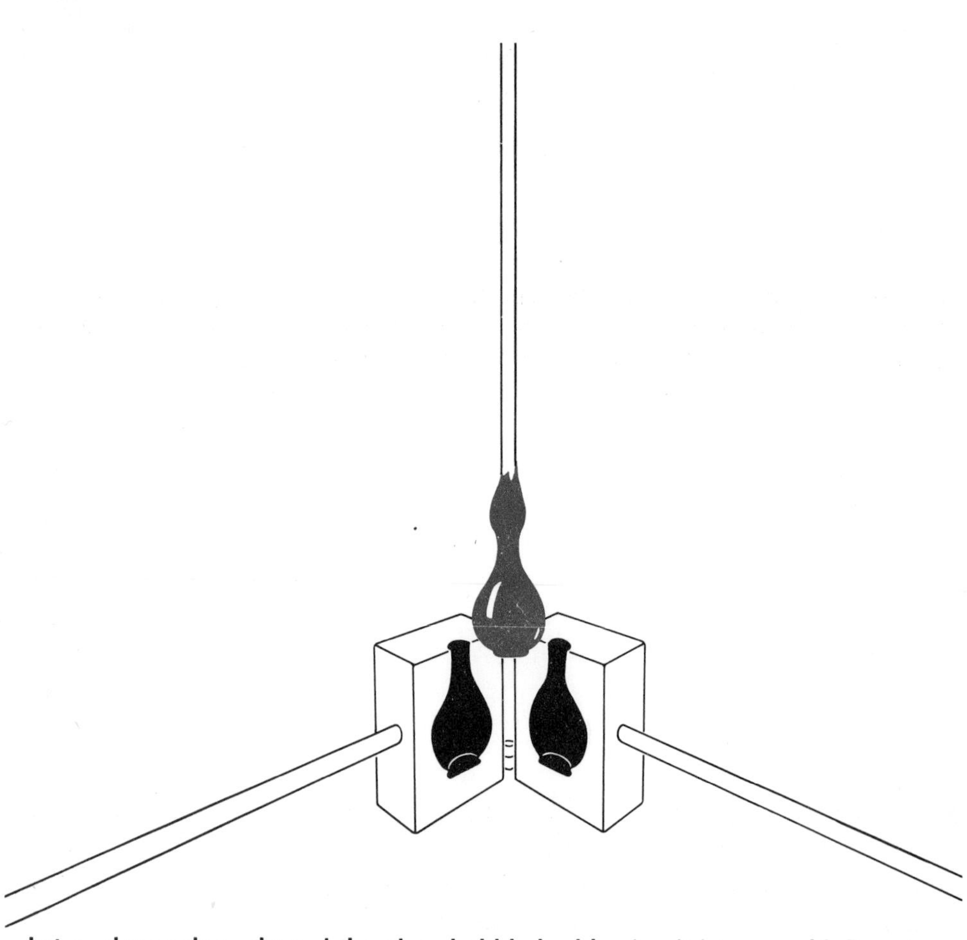

Later, glassmakers shaped the glass bubble by blowing it into a mold. By using both the mold and the blowpipe they could make more containers at less cost than ever before.

The Golden Age of Glass

After the invention of the blowpipe and with the spreading use of the mold, more and more glass was made. People discovered new uses for containers, which took on all sorts of sizes and shapes. Merchants liked the new glass jars because they did not leak. Wines, oils and honey did not taste queer, nor did perfumes evaporate from glass containers. And, what was even better, the jars and bottles could be used over and over. Traders learned that glass-packed products travelled well on long sea voyages. Alchemists, the scientists of those days, used them for chemicals and medicines. Ladies carried little bottles of perfumes and jars of cosmetics. Just as we do today, everyone admired the beauty of glass vases, goblets, bowls and bottles.

Soon there was a great demand for glass containers. When Augustus Caesar conquered Egypt in the year 31 B.C., he demanded a tribute of glass and ordered Egyptian glassmakers to come to Rome and teach his people how to make glass.

Roman and Syrian glassmakers used molds to blow "head flasks" with funny-looking faces.

HOW HAND-BLOWN GLASS IS MADE

Glass Blowing Through the Centuries

Hand-blown glass is made today in much the same way that it was in early times. Every glasshouse contains a furnace to melt the ingredients. There is always a team of glass workers. Like all good teams, everyone has a particular job to do. Each member of the team must appear in exactly the right place at exactly the right time. The head man of the team is called the "gaffer."

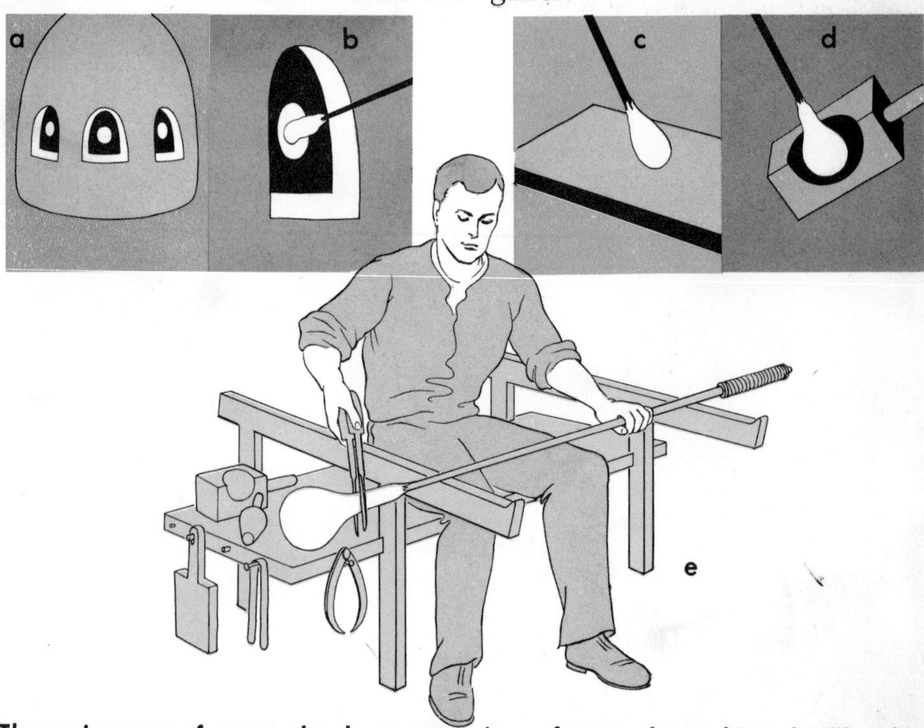

The main room of every glasshouse contains a furnace for melting the "batch" — the dry ingredients of a glass formula (a). Seated next to the "glory hole," the workman dips the blowpipe through an arch in the furnace wall into a pot of molten glass (b). Then he rolls the gob back and forth on a "marver," a flat marble or metal surface (c) to shape it. The glass bubble, called a "parison," is then put into a hollowed-out wooden block to shape it some more (d). The gaffer (e) shapes the neck of the bottle with a special tool. On pages 42 and 43 you can see how glass is blown in a modern factory.

The team works around the "glory hole," an opening in the side of the furnace. Glass must be glowing hot to be blown and shaped, so it is often reheated.

The blowpipe is a hollow iron rod, four to five feet long. One end is shaped something like a small bell. This is the "gathering end," where the glass is worked. The workman dips this end of the blowpipe through the hole in the furnace into a pot of molten glass. Turning the pipe round and round, he lifts out a gob of red-hot glass. The gob is rolled back and forth on a flat marble or metal table to give it a rough shape. Then the glass blower puffs once or twice into the blowpipe, causing a bubble to appear. This is the beginning of a bottle.

If the bottle is to be long, the workman swings the blowpipe, letting the glass droop from it like hot taffy. If the bottle is to be flat, the blowpipe is spun around. The glass bubble is now called a "parison." Putting the parison into a hollowed-out wooden block, the workman takes a few more puffs on the blowpipe and gives it to the gaffer.

The gaffer sits in a special chair, with a shelf for tools and wide arms that stick out in front. Using his left hand, he rolls the blowpipe back and forth on the arms of his chair to keep the soft glass in shape. At the same time he takes a tool with his right hand and shapes the neck. Then he lifts the blowpipe and blows the bottle.

Immediately, a helper flattens the bottom of the bottle. Another helper appears quickly with a long rod which is coated at one end with hot glass. This rod is called a "pontil." He places the glass end at the bottom of the bottle, where it melts into it.

Knocking off the blowpipe with a sharp tap, the gaffer holds the glowing-hot bottle by the pontil, cuts the rim with scissors and shapes it with a special tool. When it is finished, a helper holds the bottle with tongs while the gaffer knocks off the pontil. This leaves a scar. All hand-blown bottles have this mark, whether they were made thousands of years ago in Egypt or just last week in the United States.

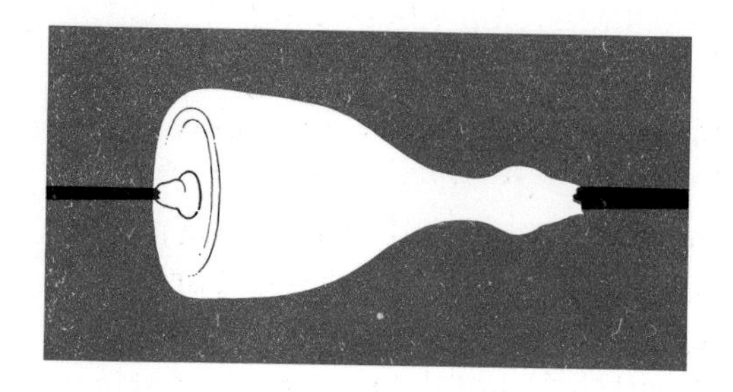

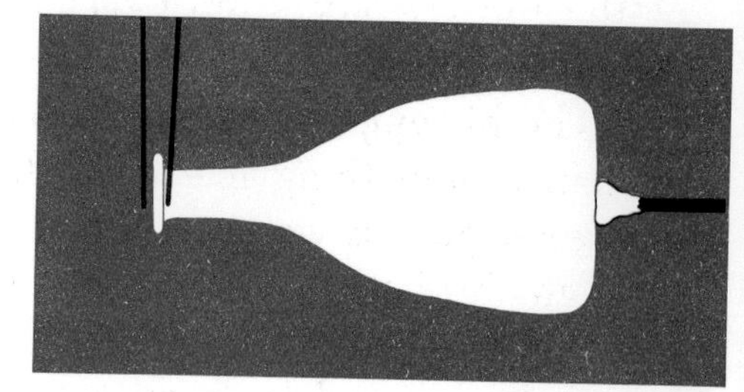

Left: The pontil has a coating of hot glass on the end, which is melted to the bottom of the bottle. Right: The rim is cut with scissors, then shaped with another special tool.

Colored Glass

The first glassmakers did not know how to make clear, transparent glass. Instead, their glass was colored and opaque. The colors in those days came from impurities in the ingredients. Their kind of glass is called "green glass." Another strange thing is that "green glass" is not always green. Sometimes it is a light yellow-brown, and sometimes it is dark brown. About 200 A.D., glassmakers learned how to take out the impurities to make clear glass. In another hundred years the first transparent glass was made for windows. We make colored glass today by mixing it with different metals. For instance, iron turns glass amber and yellow. Cobalt makes it blue. Green and blue-green come from chrome.

GLASS BECOMES POPULAR

The Second Golden Age of Glass

When Rome fell in 476 A.D., glassmakers fled to the deep forests. Though they worked in secret, not much glass was produced during the next centuries. But people continued to make it in the Near East. The first stained glass windows were made in Constantinople for a church.

As the city of Venice began to grow in wealth and power, glass became important once more. Glassmakers were highly respected and well paid. They were closely guarded, too, so that other people would not learn their secrets. The very beautiful and delicate Venetian glass was prized highly by wealthy families all over Europe. No matter how carefully glassmaking secrets were guarded, however, they were found out. It is possible that some of the glassmakers themselves sold their secrets and their skills to other nations. Anyway, by the 17th century almost every country in Europe was making glass.

In England George Ravenscroft invented a new kind of glass, called "glass-of-lead," or "flint glass," because of its ingredients. This

These remarkable bottles were blown in the Near and Middle East after the fall of Rome (A.D. 476).

In the 17th and 18th centuries, green-glass bottles were made in England for special persons. Each bottle had a glass seal with its owner's name or initials. The one on the right belonged to Jonathan Swift, author of *Gulliver's Travels*.

glass was as clear and sparkling as rock crystal, and soon earned the name of "crystal." As it was much easier to cut than most kinds of glass, much of it was decorated with cut or engraved designs. Gradually this new clear glass replaced dark glass for tableware, vases and medicine bottles.

Glassmaking Comes to America

The very first factory in the American colonies made glass, and it was a part of the first cargo shipped from the New World. This happened twelve years before the Pilgrims landed at Plymouth, Massachusetts. Does that surprise you?

In 1607 a ship sailed into Jamestown, Virginia. The colonists had waited impatiently for the boat for many weeks. The minute people saw the white sails, they stopped whatever they were doing and ran to the shore. How exciting! Here at last was news from home, far across the sea – and, best of all, a second supply of much needed food, clothing, tools, guns and gunpowder.

The ship brought more settlers as well. All but two were men. The lone women were "Mistresse Forrest and Anne Buras, Her maide," the first women to land in Jamestown. Many of the newcomers were skilled craftsmen. Among them were makers of pitch, tar, soap, clapboards and eight glassmakers.

The first glasshouse in Jamestown, Virginia, was little more than a hut. It had a main furnace and three small ones built of big rocks. Here you see one of the early glassmakers blowing a bottle.

As soon as possible, the new colonists set to work. Captain John Smith, president of the governing council of the settlement, directed the glassmakers and their helpers to select a good spot to build a glasshouse. The men needed potash and plenty of firewood to make glass. Potash was used instead of soda ash as one of its ingredients. They chose a place "in the woods neare a myle from James Towne."

The first factory was little more than a hut. It had a main furnace and three small ones built of big rocks. Although we do not know exactly what kind of glass was made in the new glasshouse, we can get an idea from pieces of green glass found in the ruins years later, which were thought to be parts of bottles and drinking glasses. It is also quite likely that glass beads were made for trade with the Indians.

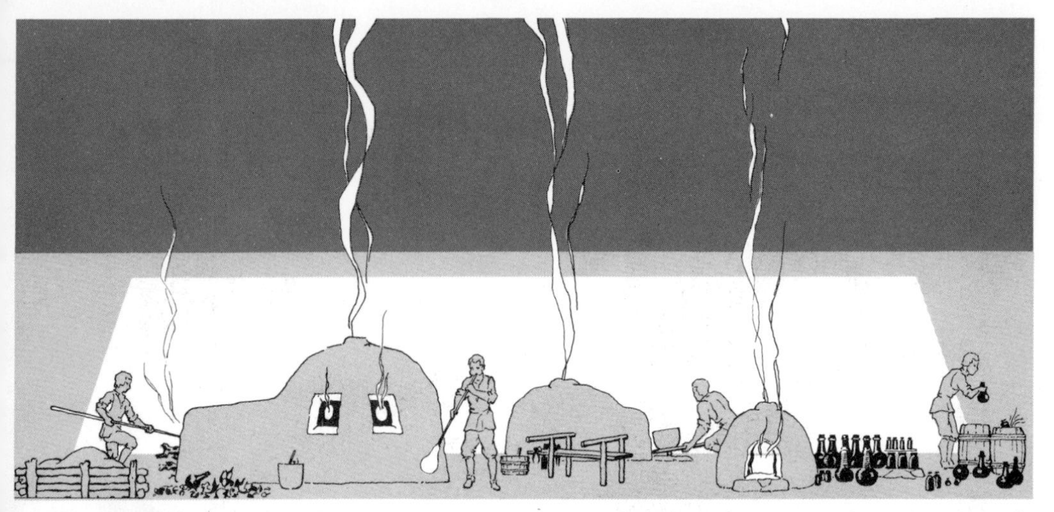

The little glasshouse in Jamestown was built a dozen years before the arrival of the pilgrims at Plymouth, Massachusetts, in 1620. It was the first factory in the New World, and glassmaking was the first industry.

Everything was fine for a time. A ship was sent to England with a cargo of pitch, tar and glass. Then one day an accident happened. Captain Smith was badly burned by a gunpowder explosion, and was forced to go back to England. Without their leader the colonists quarrelled and grew discouraged. Some were lazy and would not work, so their crops failed. Sick and weak from starvation, many of them died or were attacked by Indians. Work in the little glass factory slowed down – then stopped.

After twelve years, Captain William Norton decided to try again. Bringing six Italian glassmakers to Jamestown, he reopened the little factory in the woods. But they had a hard time. Everything went wrong. The first year a bad storm blew the roof from the glasshouse. The next year Indians attacked the settlement and massacred almost half of the colonists. It was too much for the glassmakers, who gave up and went back to Europe. This was the end of America's first industry.

Several years later, two men started a more successful glass factory in Salem, Massachusetts. The Dutch in Manhattan also made glass. However, the first really successful glass industry was started by Caspar Wistar in southern New Jersey. This was in 1739.

Wistar made all sorts of glassware, from window glass to bottles of all sizes. Many of his big bottles were used to smuggle molasses from the West Indies to America. Molasses was one of the things that was taxed highly by the British.

Wistar's glass was made in many beautiful colors. At that time fashionable ladies carried little scent bottles tucked in their gloves. Martha Washington used one of these tiny bottles. It was turquoise-blue flecked with yellow.

Caspar Wistar made many different kinds of bottles. Some of the big ones were used to smuggle molasses from the West Indies to America.

Another famous glassmaker, William Henry Stiegel, started to make glass in 1765. Like Wistar, Stiegel was born in Germany and came to this country as a young man. He was a dashing, animated person, and was nicknamed "Baron."

The "Baron" did everything in a grand manner. Building a big glass plant at Manheim, Pennsylvania, he hired the best glassmakers he could find. They came from all over Europe. At one time there were as many as 130 men working busily in his plant.

Stiegel's glassware was beautiful. He made hundreds of different kinds of containers. There were ink bottles, mustard jars, flasks,

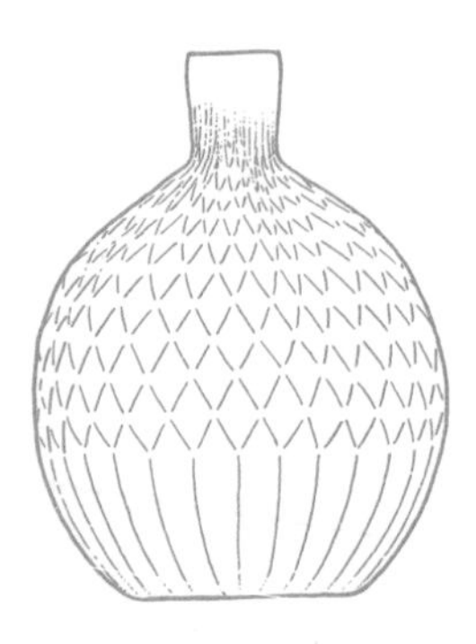

One of the earliest American glassmakers to be successful, Stiegel built a plant in Pennsylvania in 1765. Here are three of the "Baron's" bottles, made of beautiful cut glass.

decanters, cruets, tumblers — almost every kind of bottle you can think of. There were clear glass bottles and colored bottles. Many were cut and etched with lovely designs. Some were ornamented with gilt. But, unfortunately for the "Baron," it was not long before he ran heavily into debt. In 1774 he landed in debtor's prison.

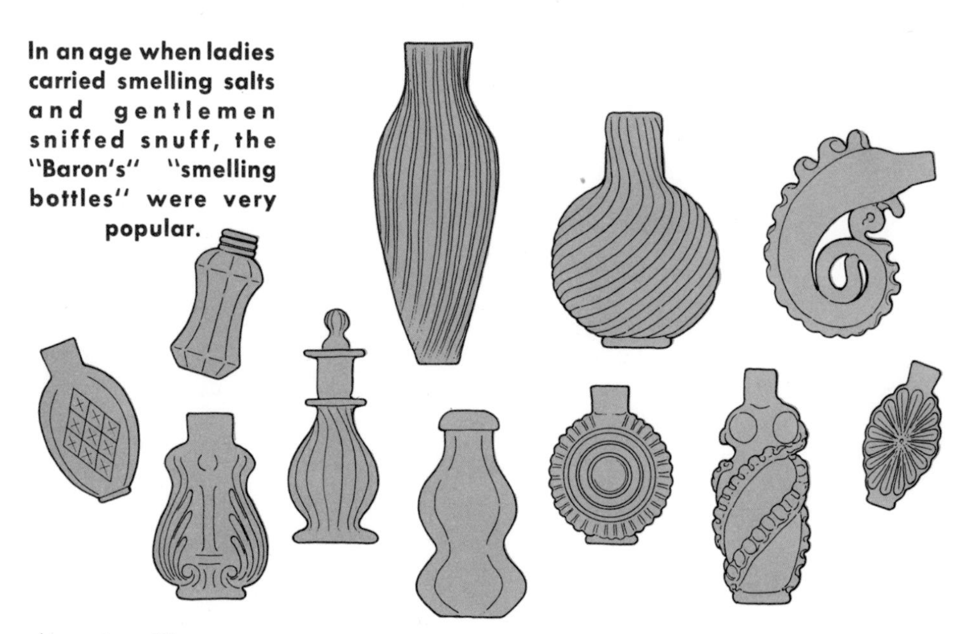
In an age when ladies carried smelling salts and gentlemen sniffed snuff, the "Baron's" "smelling bottles" were very popular.

America Grows

After the Revolution, glass was made in Connecticut, Maryland and New Jersey. In 1797 coal was found near Pittsburgh, Pennsylvania. This important discovery led to the beginning of the big Pittsburgh glass industry. Until this time glass furnaces had always burned tremendous amounts of wood. Here was a new and plentiful source of fuel. Gradually coal replaced wood for the hot fires of the glass furnaces.

As the United States began to expand, canals connected the great rivers, which became busy highways. Roads were built across mountains and plains. Railroads came into being, and new cities sprang up. The growth of the nation created a greater demand for glass. The glassmakers moved westward, knowing that wherever they went they could get a job.

About this time another type of bottle was made. This was the "Memorial" bottle. Americans have always been proud of their heritage, and the glassmakers took this way to remember heroes and important events. These beautifully colored bottles were blown into

Ludlow bottles appeared in the 18th and 19th centuries. Because they were made by the free-blown method, they were often crudely formed.

These flasks were known as Pitkin flasks. The type originated in the Pitkin Glass Works, and was later produced in eastern and midwestern glasshouses during the 18th and early 19th centuries.

The lily pad pattern was a popular design in the 1850's.

Chestnut flasks were molded in patterns of ribbed and diamond designs.

Midwestern glasshouses produced swirled jugs and bottles in the early 19th century.

The size of early American bottles varied greatly. Some held as much as 20 gallons.

These are some of the different kinds of bottles that were popular in America at an early date.

carved molds. The most popular design was the American Eagle. Next was the portrait of George Washington. Benjamin Franklin, John Quincy Adams and other famous persons were honored also. There were bottles to celebrate the opening of a canal, the first railroads, steamboats, and, during the gold rush—"For Pike's Peak."

New Uses for Glass

As glass grew more popular, still more uses for it were found. First came the nursing bottle, then the Mason jar with its tight screw-on cap. Dr. Hervey Thatcher perfected the first milk bottle.

Before the milk bottle was invented, families living in cities and towns had milk delivered on horse-drawn wagons. Housewives brought pitchers and pails to the wagons to be filled with milk from big cans. Those who came first got all the cream, because cream floats to the top. They did not always get the right measure, either. In the hot summer, flies swarmed around the sweet-smelling milk. Dust and germs from the dirty streets settled on the open containers. So many people became sick that Dr. Thatcher was worried. He decided to do something about it, and invented the milk bottle. How fortunate we are today to have our milk delivered to us in sanitary, tightly-sealed bottles! And we are always sure of getting the right amount of cream and the right measure.

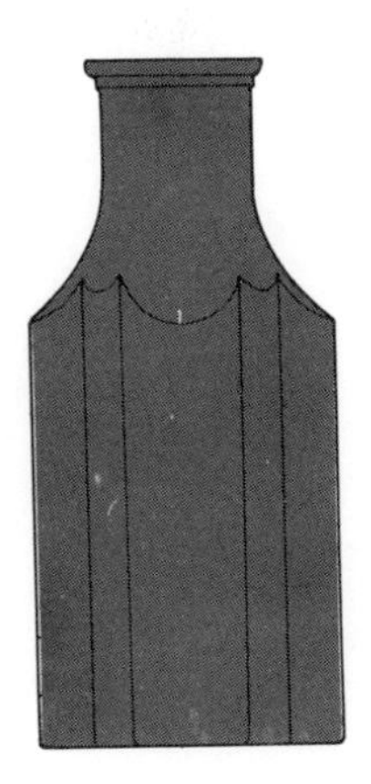

Even ordinary pickle jars were molded in attractive shapes and decorated with elaborate designs.

This is a glass factory in the United States during the days of the Civil War. An apprentice worked many long years before he was allowed to touch a blowpipe.

Until the early 19th century, the only way to preserve food had been by salting or drying. Then, in France, Nicolas Appert had an idea. Why not put fresh foods into glass jars, then seal and cook them? He tried it, and found that it worked! Furthermore, the food tasted good! This was the start of the canning industry.

Have you ever wondered why we call the preserving of food "canning"? In those days tin containers were called "canisters." This was a long word for the bookkeepers to write, so they shortened it to "can." Today canning means to sterilize and preserve food in airtight containers, whether the containers are made of tin or glass, and whether the process is done in factories or at home.

The first food to be preserved in glass in the United States was canned in 1819. In Boston, they packed fruits, pickles and sauces, and in New York were packed the first fish and shellfish.

GLASS IN THE 20th CENTURY

Recent Improvements in Glassmaking

Throughout the centuries there had been improvements in glassmaking. New ingredients created new kinds of glass. Furnaces were better. New fuels – oil and gas – were cheaper and easier to control. But glass was still blown by lung power, much as it had been for 2,000 years, and this method was too slow. The very most that a glassmaker and his helpers could make in a day was about 240 bottles. This may sound like a lot of bottles, but it was not nearly enough. Glassmakers began to think of ways to make more. After a while, a machine was developed to blow glass by air pressure. Although this helped, the glassmakers were not satisfied. They continued to experiment.

In 1903 Michael Owens perfected the fully automatic bottle machine. Here was real progress! One of these machines with its many metal arms and compressed air was able to do the work of dozens of glass blowers and their helpers. Soon this machine was turning out an amazing number of bottles – one million bottles a week!

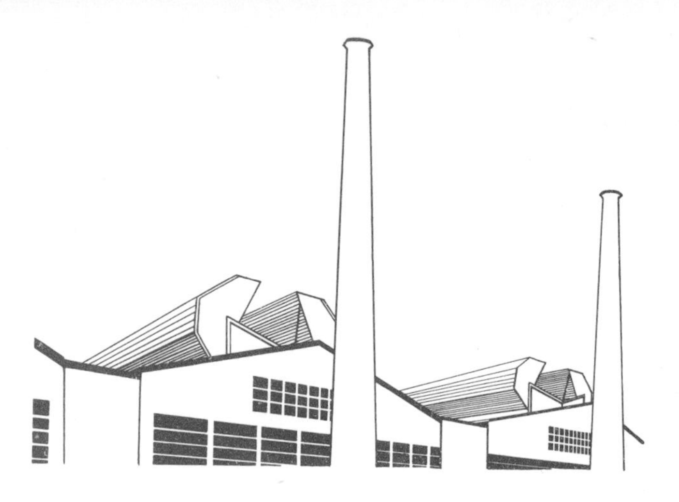

How Modern Glass Is Made

The ordinary glass that we use every day is made from three main ingredients. The first is pure, clean *sand*. This sand is mostly silica or quartz. The second ingredient is *soda ash* (soda carbonate). The third is *limestone*. "Cullet" (crushed glass) is added to make the ingredients more workable. Small quantities of other substances are used. Some help the mixture to melt faster. Some make the finished glass stronger, or keep it from being dull or opaque, while others give it color.

Glass ingredients are measured as carefully as a druggist measures medicine. A recipe is followed, so that each ingredient is exactly right to the very ounce. This is done on automatic scales.

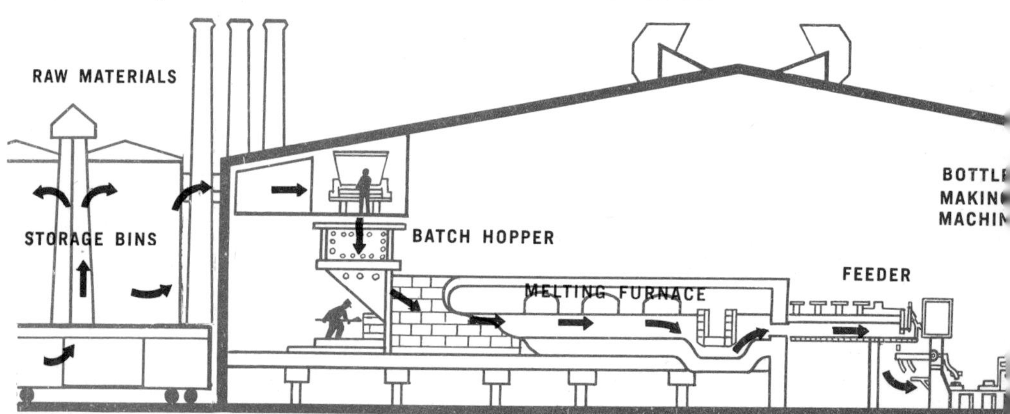

Today glass factories are large. Raw materials come by truck, railroad and boat. They are stored in huge bins until they are needed. After the ingredients are weighed, they are mixed for about four minutes in a giant "hopper." This mixture is called a "batch," and weighs thousands of pounds. The batch is fed into the furnace on an endless belt, or in buckets that travel on overhead rails.

The glass furnace is really an enormous melting pot. There are two kinds, the pot furnace and the tank furnace. Optical glass is made in a pot furnace. Glass for bottles, jars and light bulbs is made in the tank type. The fire in a tank furnace is forced through openings in the walls. It burns *over* the batch. The heat is terrific – over 2700 degrees Fahrenheit! No wonder scientists doubt that early Phoenicians made glass over an ordinary outdoor fire. The furnace never stops. It runs day and night, week after week. Although it is made of a special heat-resistant material, it actually burns itself out in about two years.

The batch starts to melt almost immediately. As it begins to boil, it bubbles furiously and glows white-hot. The molten glass moves in a slow, steady current through the tank. This is something like the currents in the ocean or those in the air. Here it is caused by hotter and cooler parts of the tank. When the glass is thoroughly melted it flows into a chamber to be refined. The impurities rise to the top and are held back, while the glass flows on into the automatic feeder.

Follow the arrows in the diagram to see how glass bottles are made today.

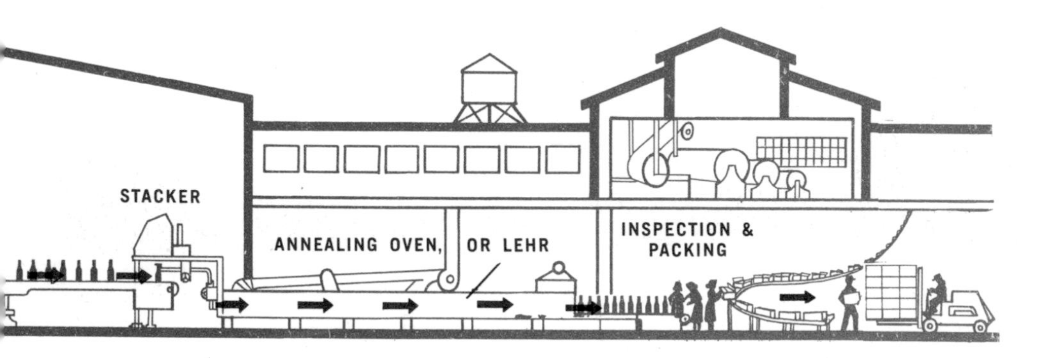

In a modern glass factory, raw materials are stored in huge bins. After the ingredients are weighed and mixed, the "batch" travels to the furnace on a long belt.

The molten glass inside the furnace is very hot — over 2700 degrees Fahrenheit!

The operator in the batch department checks his control panel.

There are two kinds of feeders. In one, molds on the arms of the glass-blowing machine dip into the molten glass, and each mold sucks up the right amount of glass. In the other, the red-hot material goes into a trough, and is pushed through a hole in the bottom. Then the gob of hot glass drops into a mold on the end of an arm. Here it is pressed into a rough shape. The mold opens, and quicker than a

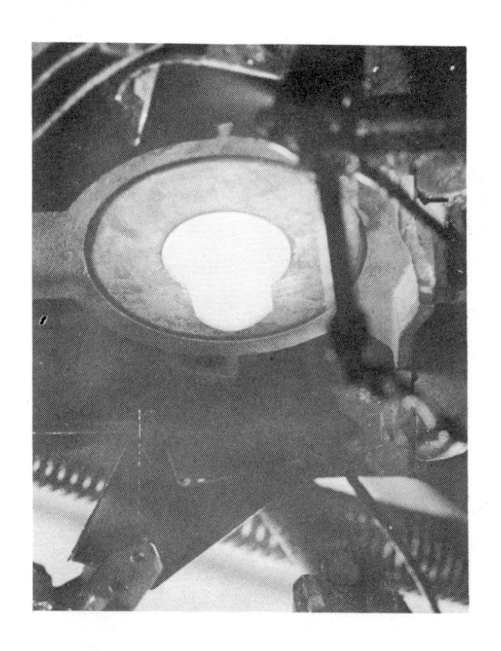

Red-hot gobs, about the consistency of taffy, are cut free by mechanical shears and dropped into a waiting mold.

Compressed air from a finishing mold gives a glass container its final shape.

magician can say "presto chango," another mold catches the glass. Swish! Compressed air comes through the hollow arm of the mold. The jaws open, and there is a bottle! It sounds easy, doesn't it? However, the automatic bottle machines are very complicated. They have as many as fifteen arms, each with a mold. Sometimes the arms are on a circular machine that turns like a carousel. On other machines the arms move straight along. It is very important that each container be just like the one before it. The next time you go to the grocery store, look at a row of pickles or jellies. All the jars with the same label are exactly alike. You cannot tell them apart.

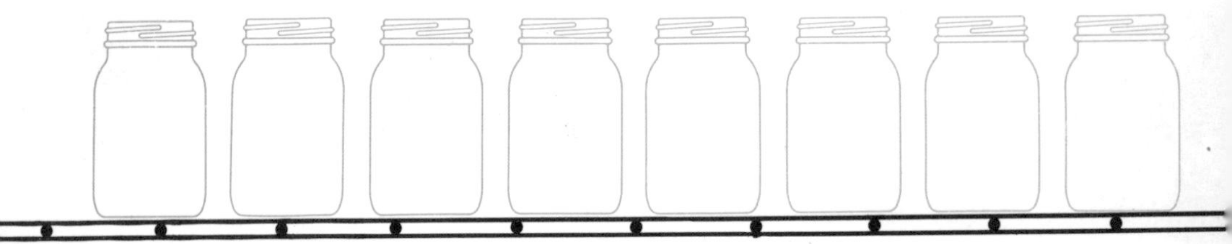

Now let's see what happens after the bottle is made. It is still red-hot when it comes from the automatic blowing machine, and must be cooled very slowly. Glass becomes brittle if it cools too fast, and if you were to touch it, it might suddenly fly into smithereens. So a "knock-off arm" sends the container onto a conveyor belt, which takes it into an "annealing lehr," or cooling oven. The lehr is like a long tunnel. Extremely hot at one end, it gradually gets cooler and cooler. An endless parade of red-hot bottles enters the hot end and comes out at the other end cool enough to touch.

And still there is more to be done. Now the bottle must be inspected, packaged and shipped. Inspection is most important. Each container that is not perfect is sent back to be broken into cullet. Other tests are made, too. At each different process samples are taken and sent to the laboratory to be tested. This shows whether the molten glass is exactly right, and whether adjustments should be made in molding, blowing or cooling.

Every year bottle machines supply billions and billions of bottles and jars to hold food we eat and the beverages we drink. Billions more hold our medicines, drugs, serums and chemicals. Do you know how many glass containers are made in one year? *Eighteen billion!* Glass bottles and jars are strong, tough and durable, so they can be used over and over. Being smooth and hard, they are easy to wash and sterilize. Since glass has no odor, it cannot give things a strange taste. Mass production has lowered the costs of these containers, and we know that things packed and well sealed in glass are safe, sanitary and well preserved.

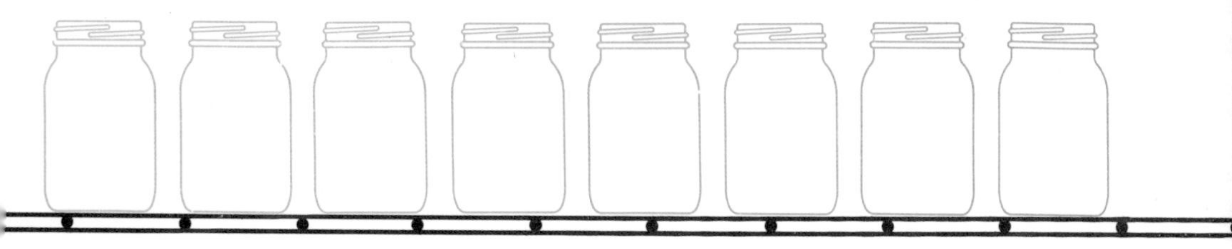

A "knock-off arm" places the bottles on a conveyor belt. This takes them through an annealing lehr where they are cooled slowly.

To protect its contents, every glass container must be perfect. All are examined for flaws before they are packed. A bottle or jar with even the tiniest flaw is discarded.

The New Glass Age

The art of glassmaking always has been a mystery to most people. Perhaps this is because glassmakers were proud of their skill and kept their methods a deep, dark secret. No one but the glassmakers themselves knew how the glass was made. These secrets were treasured and guarded. They often were handed down from father to son – generation after generation. Legends, stories and superstitions about glass added to its air of mystery.

The 20th century has seen many changes. Glassmaking is no longer a secret, nor is glass a luxury, for it has become an everyday substance. If the early glassmakers could see our many modern uses for glass, they would find it hard to believe their eyes.

All modern glass is not the same. There are many different kinds, each with its own particular use. The main ingredient usually is silica, but scientists and glassmakers have found that they can make various types of glass by adding other substances.

Optical glass (the kind used in eyeglasses), for instance, is very special. It is almost pure, for it must be perfect and without bubbles or streaks. It must be strong enough to resist strain. After it is shaped, ground and polished into all sorts of lenses, optical glass helps millions of persons to see better.

Another kind of glass – *architectural glass,* used for building purposes – plays an important part in our modern life. The big picture windows for our homes and the huge plate-glass windows for stores are made from this glass. Office buildings, stores and factories use glass building blocks and fire-resistant wire glass partitions. Architectural glass is used for ornamental purposes, too. Many public buildings have glass fronts. Sculpture and beautiful stained glass windows are made of this material.

Corning Glass Works

Corning's new 28-story skyscraper in New York City dramatically uses glass as an architectural material.

Owens-Corning Fiberglas Corporation

Left: Fiberglas is made in a modern factory. The material in the picture is being fed into an oven where the fibers will be heat-set in a crimped position. Right: These drapes are one of many beautiful products made of Fiberglas. Fiberglas is soft and easy to take care of, fireproof and thoroughly washable.

As you know, molten glass is much like hot taffy or molasses candy. It can be pulled out into long threads. These glass threads are called *fibers,* and sometimes *spun glass.* Glass fibers are made into many things, depending on the thickness of the fibers. Glass mineral wool is made of coarse fibers. This is made into thick blankets, boards or blocks, and is used to insulate homes, refrigerators, ovens, pipes and batteries. Because glass is a poor conductor of electricity, glass mineral wool is used to insulate electric wires and cables. Extra fine glass fibers are spun into yarn or thread. As they are flexible, they can be woven into cloth. Cloth of glass shines like silk and is used to make draperies, shower curtains, tablecloths and lamp shades. Sometimes glass threads are combined with other kinds of thread and used in men's ties or in women's hats.

Safety glass is also remarkable glass made in several different ways. In one way, wire mesh is embedded in the glass. In others, plastics are pressed between layers of glass like a sandwich. Still another kind is made shatterproof by a heat treatment.

Steuben Glass

Designing and engraving glass for decorative purposes is a true art. The three sections of this handsome glass totem pole represent the Indians of North, South and Central America.

This is how a fine piece of glass is blown in a modern factory. A team of men work together around the the glory hole.

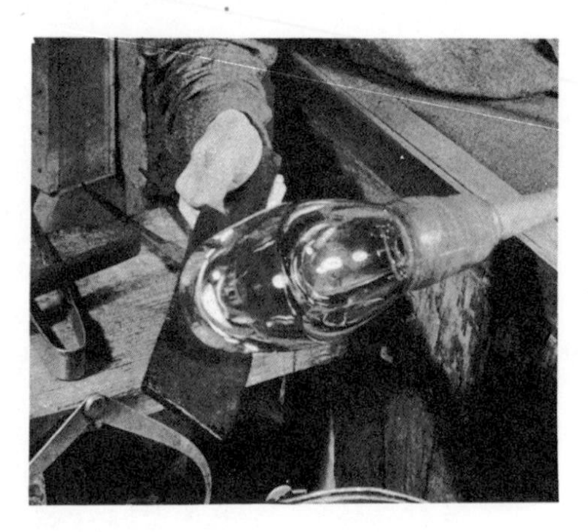

Left: The gatherer blows the glass. Above: Another worker, called a "servitor," begins to shape the glass.

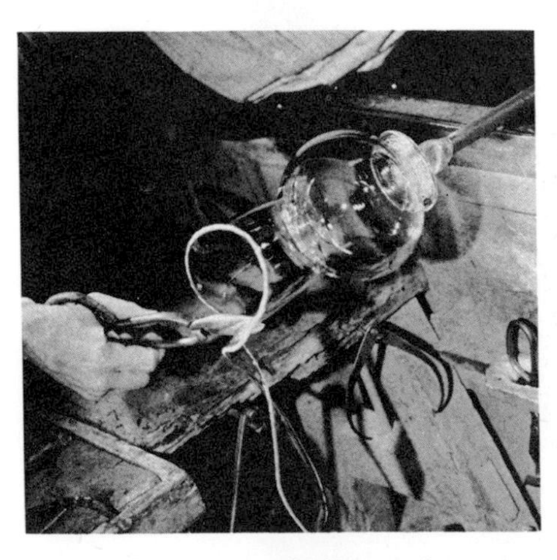

The gaffer joins and shapes the parts of the glass piece.

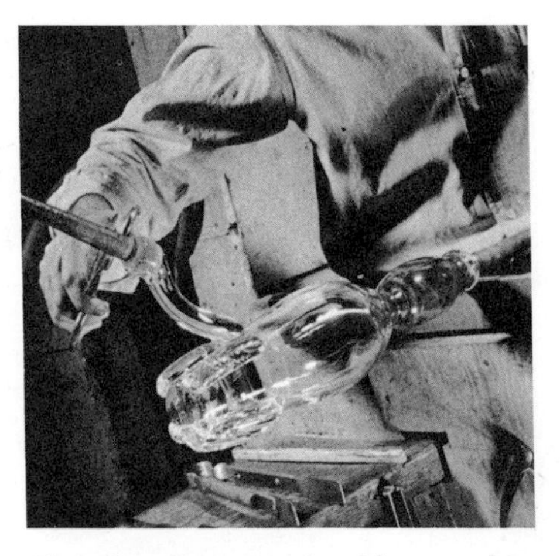

Then he decorates it with extra bits of glass.

The gaffer must reheat the piece frequently to maintain a proper working temperature during the final opening out and shaping of the glass.

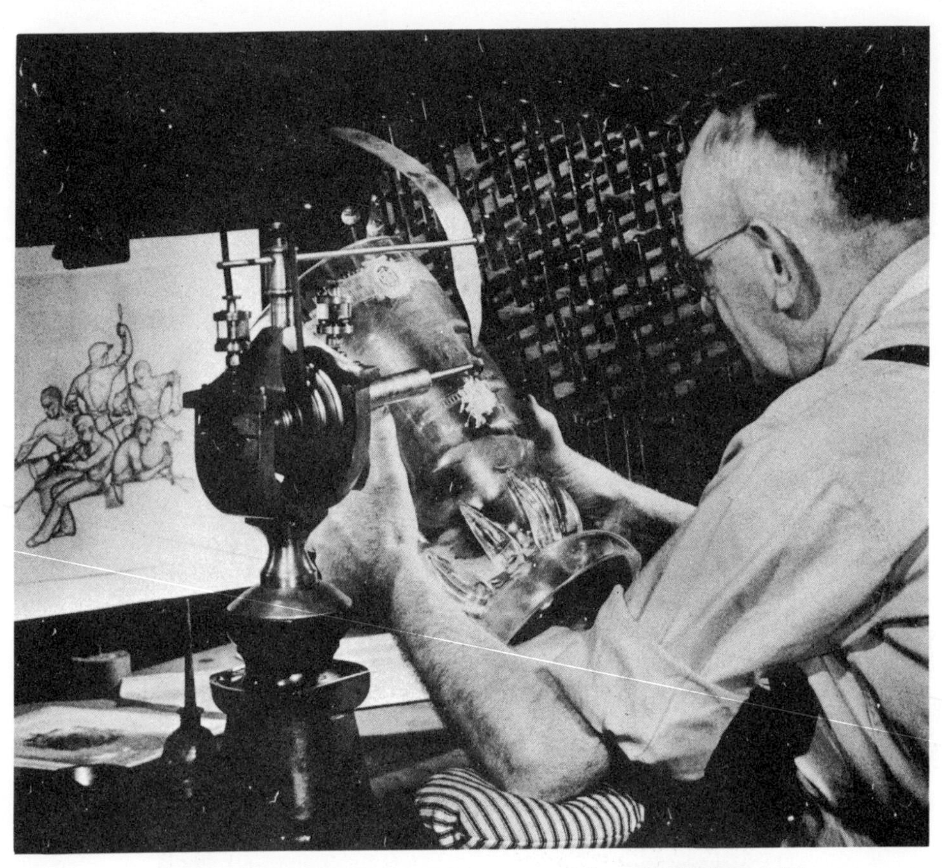

Copper wheel engraving calls for a skillful eye and a steady hand. The engraver works at a small lathe into which he fits copper wheels of varying thicknesses and diameters. To make the design, the glass is pressed against the revolving wheel which is fed with a rough mixture.

Photograph of Steuben glass by Herbert Smit

The circus scene on this beautiful vase was designed by Bruce Moore, a noted American sculptor.

Photograph of Baccarat crystal by Agneta Fisher

Combining beauty with function, today's lovely drinking glasses are a far cry from the first rough glass arrowheads.

Glass ovenware can stand great temperature changes, and is used to make Mother's pie pans and oven dishes. It is made like ordinary glass, except that it is kept hot for a long time when it comes from the furnace. Then a glass pan, for example, is dipped into chemicals that eat away all the substances but silica. This process leaves hundreds of tiny holes. The glass pan is reheated until the glass melts into the holes and closes them, causing the glass to shrink.

The most beautiful glass of our modern world is perhaps that

The graceful shapes and intricate patterns of these glasses enhance the liquids they hold.

Photograph of Baccarat crystal by Agneta Fisher

which is made into tableware, vases and bowls. Lovely designs sometimes are cut or engraved on this glassware, which often costs thousands of dollars. This is because particular bowls or vases are designed by artists and made by specially skilled craftsmen, so that this glass is truly "fit for a king."

The next time you drink a glass of water or select a bottle of your favorite drink, remember the story of glass. Think of the thousands of years it took glassmakers to develop the glass we know today, and think of the many wonderful things that glass does for us.

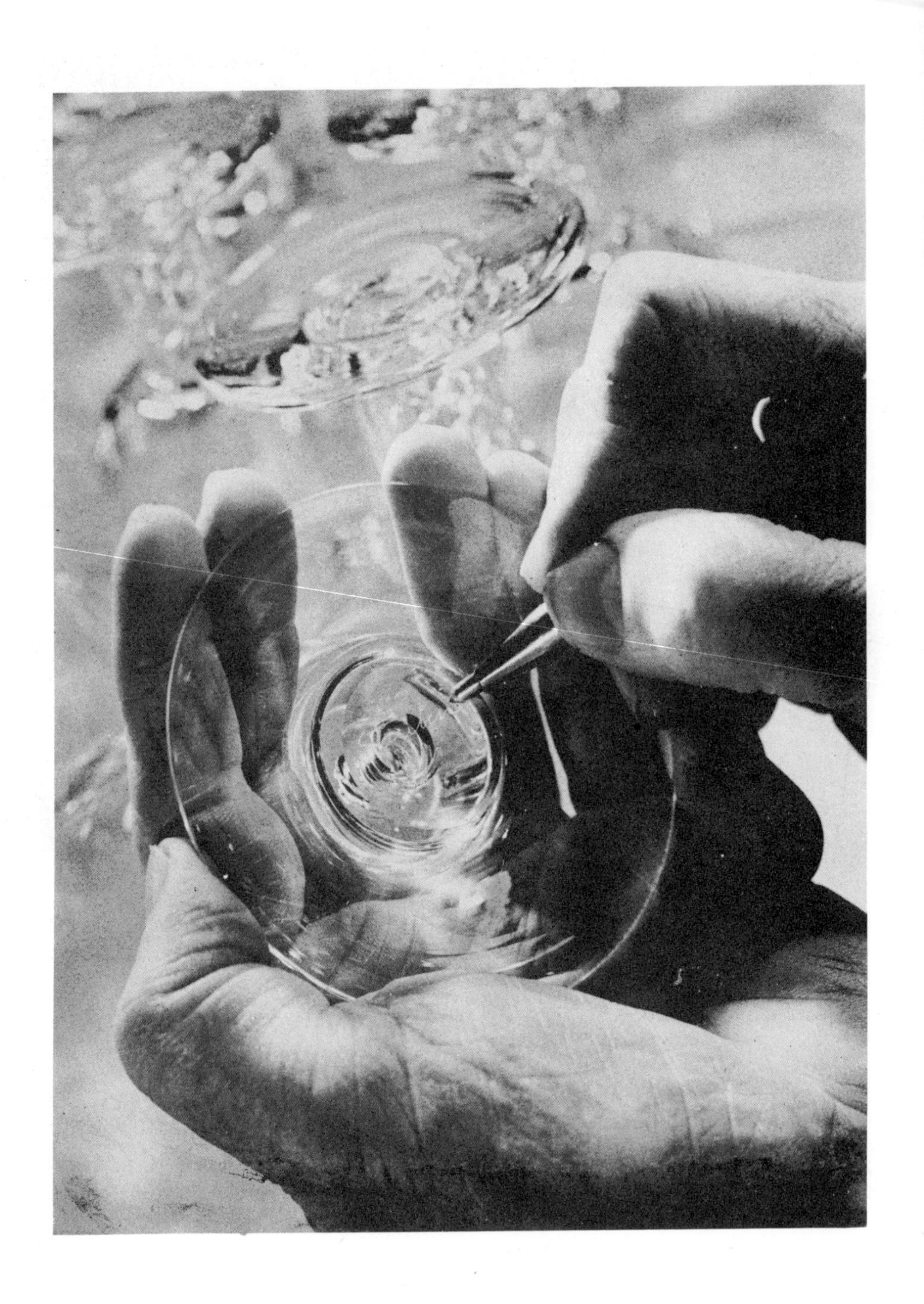